STEVE PARISH · **WILDFLOWERS** · AUSTRALIA FROM THE HEART

Contents

AUSTRALIA FROM THE HEART

The flowering part of a wild plant is really nothing more than a means of achieving fertilisation to produce seeds for a new generation, and this "motivation" is behind the many distinctive looks that plants have evolved – looks that must attract animals, the main agents for pollen transfer. Inducements offered by plants include food, nesting materials and places to rest or lay eggs. This drive to find pollinators has brought about the enormous variety of distinctive Australian plants.

Being voiceless, flowers have evolved colours, scents, shapes, patterns and textures that appeal to an animal's senses. I am a visual person, and it is the flowering features of plants that have intrigued and often awed me for many years. Through this gift book, I hope the joy of my discoveries lights a flame in your heart.

Steve Parish

Title page: Gungurru, *Eucalyptus caesia.*
Previous pages: Many-flowered Fringe Lily, *Thysanotus multiflorus.*
Left: One of the flame peas, *Chorizema retrorsum.*

Armed with strategies developed in isolation over millions of years, flowering plants have spread throughout Australia, from mountain top to river valley, from seashore to inland plain. Australia's climate, landforms and geology create a host of environments that provide the sunlight, water, soil and space necessary for plants to grow.

As a place to live, however, the continent seems inhospitable. Its ancient soils are poor in nutrients. Humid environments are limited: 70% of the country is considered arid or semi-arid. The dry, temperate habitats that dominate Australia are also fire-prone.

Yet some 18 500 species of flowering plants manage to thrive on what the country has to offer. Adaptability and diversification have been key factors in the remarkable success of Australian flowering plants. Millions of years of dynamic evolutionary processes have equipped plants, such as acacias and eucalypts, with various mechanisms to reduce water loss, recover from fire and even fix nitrogen in the soil. With the added benefits of diversity, some groups, such as grevilleas, have representatives in most habitats, wet or dry, tropical or temperate.

Honey Grevillea and ephemeral flowers bring mulga scrubland to life in central Australia.

Red and Green Kangaroo Paw in foreground, Kings Park, Perth, WA.

Yellow daisies (*Asteraceae* family), Mt Augustus National Park, WA.

Coastal heath at Nambung National Park, WA.

Scarlet Banksia (*Banksia coccinea*), Stirling Range National Park, WA.

THE WONDROUS WORLD OF COLOUR

Colour adds much to the beauty of Australian wildflowers. The saturated red of Sturt's Desert Pea, the intense yellow of wattle blossom, the stunning blue of a Scented Sun Orchid, all leap out from sun-bleached backgrounds and demand attention.

Different arrangements of tiny pigment cells in plant sap reflect and absorb light differently, producing colours of varying intensity. Some flowers have no pigment cells, and air between the colourless petals creates an illusion of white.

Wildflower colours attract animal pollinators. The colours that delight the human eye go largely unseen by insects, which pollinate nearly 80% of flowering plants. Where humans see red, most insects see black because they have ultraviolet vision: yellow, blue and ultraviolet combine to form many colours invisible to humans.

Some birds, mammals and butterflies have red-sensitive vision, and so Australia's many red-hued flowers appeal to these important pollinators. Flower colour has benefits aside from pollination. Sunscreening purple pigments protect delicate tissues from those same ultraviolet rays that make flowers attractive to insects.

Kangaroo paw, everlasting daisies, peaflowers and dampiera mass together in Kings Park, Perth, WA.

11

Lazy Spider Orchid, *Caladenia multiclavia.*

Purple Flag, *Patersonia occidentalis*, against everlasting daisies, *Rhodanthe chlorocephala rosea*.

Mountain Devil, *Lambertia formosa*.

A peaflower, family *Fabaceae*, of which Australia has about 1100 species.

Cowslip Orchids, *Caladenia flava*.

Sturt's Desert Pea, *Swainsona formosa.*

Cape York Lily, *Curcuma australasica.*

Bell-fruited Mallee, *Eucalyptus preissiana*.

Western Bloodwood, *Eucalyptus terminalis*.

Albany Blackbutt, *Eucalyptus staeri.*

Graceful Cassia, *Senna venusta.*

Lilac Hibiscus, *Alyogyne huegelii.*

Scented Sun Orchid, *Thelymitra aristata*.

Massed dampiera and daisy species.

Tasmanian Heath, *Epacris* sp.

The element of texture adds much to the visual beauty of wildflowers. Humans are very sensitive to touch, and the textures of flowers evoke comparisons with familiar objects: papery everlasting daisies, bristly bottlebrushes, furry kangaroo paws, and so on.

Texture, or lustre, comes from the structure of the individual parts of a flower. If the petal surface is smooth, a flower looks shiny or metallic. The mirror effect of a starch layer within a petal makes a flower shine too. Hairy or warty surfaces produce a matt or velvet effect. A waxy surface film dulls a petal's lustre and tones down its colours.

Texture enhances the attractiveness to an animal of a flower's colour and shape. Grooves in petals guide tongues seeking nectar. It can also deceive: male Thynnid wasps try to mate with Drakaea orchids because the flowers look, smell and feel like the female wasp.

Texture plays other strategic roles in plant survival. Hairy petals insulate delicate tissues; waxy ones reduce water loss … and the rustle of everlasting daisies, making them sound as though they're dead, just might save them from browsing plant eaters.

Massed wattle blossom. All the wattles are acacias, members of the *Mimosaceae* family.

Poached Egg Daisy, *Polycalymma stuartii*.

Pink Everlasting Daisy, *Rhodanthe chlorocephala* var. *rosea*.

Wallum Fringe Lily, *Nymphoides exiliflora.*

Desert Peaflower, *Swainsona maccullochiana.*

Mottlecah, *Eucalyptus macrocarpa*.

Purple Enamel Orchid, *Elythranthera brunonis.*

Crimson Kunzea, *Kunzea baxteri.*

Basket Flower, *Adenanthos obovatus*.

Rose Coneflower, *Isopogon formosus*.

Broad-leaved Parakeelya, *Calandrinia balonensis*.

Extreme close-up of a Southern Plains Banksia, *Banksia media*.

Giant Water Lily, *Nymphaea gigantea.*

Swamp Orchid, *Phaius tancarvilleae.*

A GALLERY OF SHAPES

For centuries flowers have been an inspiration to artists, artisans and architects who have used stylised flower shapes as symbolic and decorative motifs. Australian wildflowers are no exception, appearing on everything from the national coat of arms to bed-linen.

A flower's shape can help a plant to protect its reproductive organs. Shape also facilitates fertilisation by being suited to particular animals' vision and ways of gathering food.

Flowers range in shape from simple, flat circles through bells and tubes to complex, bizarre shapes, such as those of orchids that resemble insects, mushrooms and even dung.

New dimensions are added to form when basic flower shapes appear in massed arrangements called inflorescences. Again, the variety is immense, but, overall, the shapes are open or elongated. An everlasting daisy has a centre of small, tightly packed flowers surrounded by rows of petal-like leaves. Thousands of crowded flowers that open sequentially from bottom to top create a cone-shaped banksia spike. On a cylindrical bottlebrush spike, the flowers open at the same time. Inflorescence is common in Australian wildflowers and is especially suited to flying insects and the brush-tipped tongues of honeyeaters, lorikeets, fruit bats and honey possums.

The rare Queen of Sheba orchid, *Thelymitra variegata*.

Fringed Mantis Orchid, *Caladenia dilatata* var. *falcata.*

Cow Kicks, *Stylidium schoenoides.*

Fuchsia Heath, *Epacris longiflora.*

Mountain Grevillea, *Grevillea alpina.*

Cranbrook Bell, *Darwinia meeboldii*.

Eremophila, *Eremophila maculata* var. *brevifolia*.

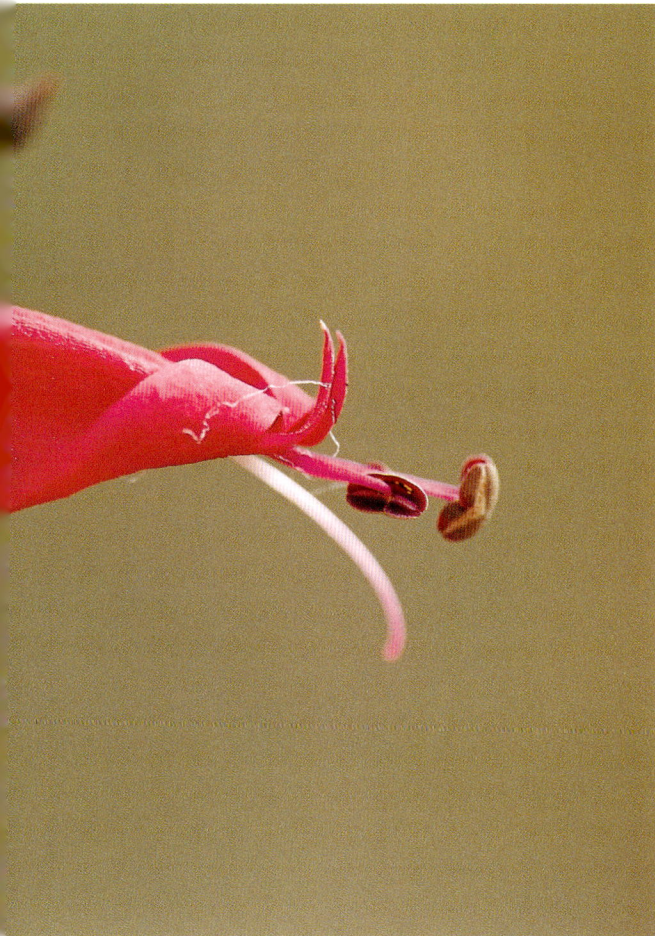

Red and Green Kangaroo Paw, *Anigozanthos manglesii*.

Victorian Heath, *Epacris impressa.*

Cooktown Orchid, *Dendrobium bigibbum.*

Cat's Whisker, *Orthosiphon aristatus.*

Native Rhododendron, *Rhododendron lochae*.

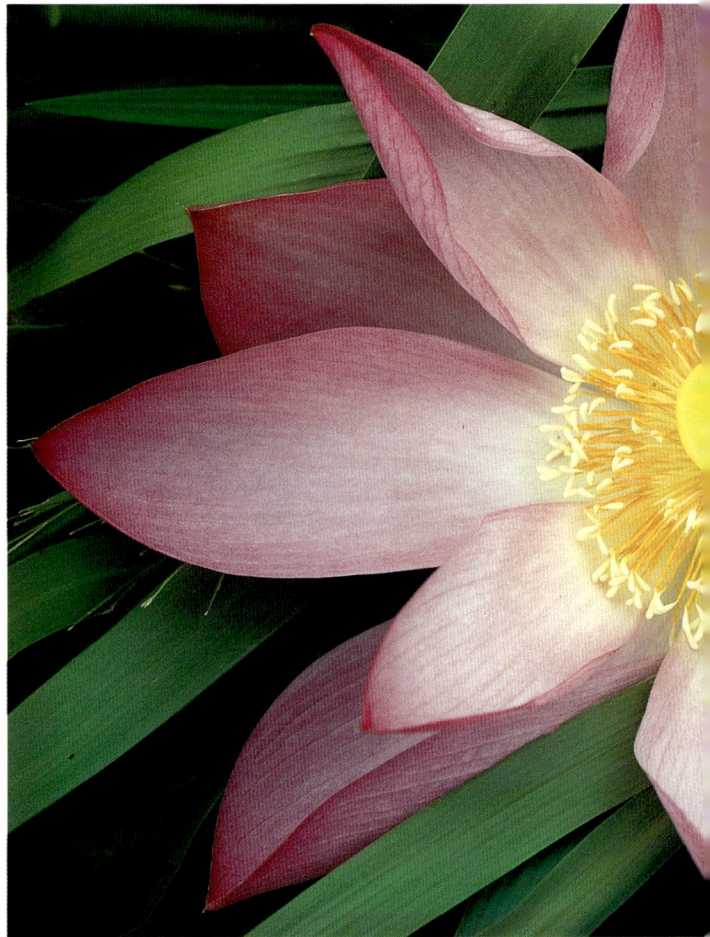

Overhead view of a Lotus Lily, *Nelumbo nucifera*.

Scallops, *Hakea cucullata*.

Tinsel Flower, *Cyanostegia corifolia*.

A grevillea flower spike.

Cassia flowers, one of the subspecies of *Senna artemisioides*.

FINDING A PATTERN

There are endless patterns in the repetitions, sequences and contrasts of wildflower shapes and colours. But pattern, like beauty, is in the eye of the beholder. For insects with ultraviolet vision, special guide marks appear on nearly half of all flowers. The human eye can see those contrasting lines, dots and patches in only about half of all those cases.

Combinations of guide marks, colours and shapes create patterns that the insect brain registers and stores. Pattern helps an insect to see a target flower from far away, home in on the flower's centre, and claim a food reward in exchange for dropping off and picking up pollen.

Converging lines along flower petals are a common guide mark. These are usually a dark or contrasting colour, but can be grooves. Contrasting petal tips and a dark central patch on a wide, flat flower produce a pattern of concentric circles. To an insect, the spots on the inner surface of a tubular flower resemble stamens and are an invitation to investigate. When guide marks change colour after fertilisation, insects stop visiting because their stored image does not fit the flower's new pattern.

When a flower pattern is so specialised that it attracts only one kind of pollinator, the plant has no chance of reproducing if the pollinator fails to appear during flowering time.

Pink Rice Flower, *Pimelea ferruginea*.

Geraldton Wax, *Chamelaucium uncinatum.*

Swamp Daisy, *Actinodium cunninghamii*, one of Australia's 1400 species of Myrtaceae.

Sturt's Desert Rose, *Gossypium sturtianum*, floral emblem of the NT.

Rose Mallee, *Eucalyptus rhodantha*.

Pentachondra pamila.

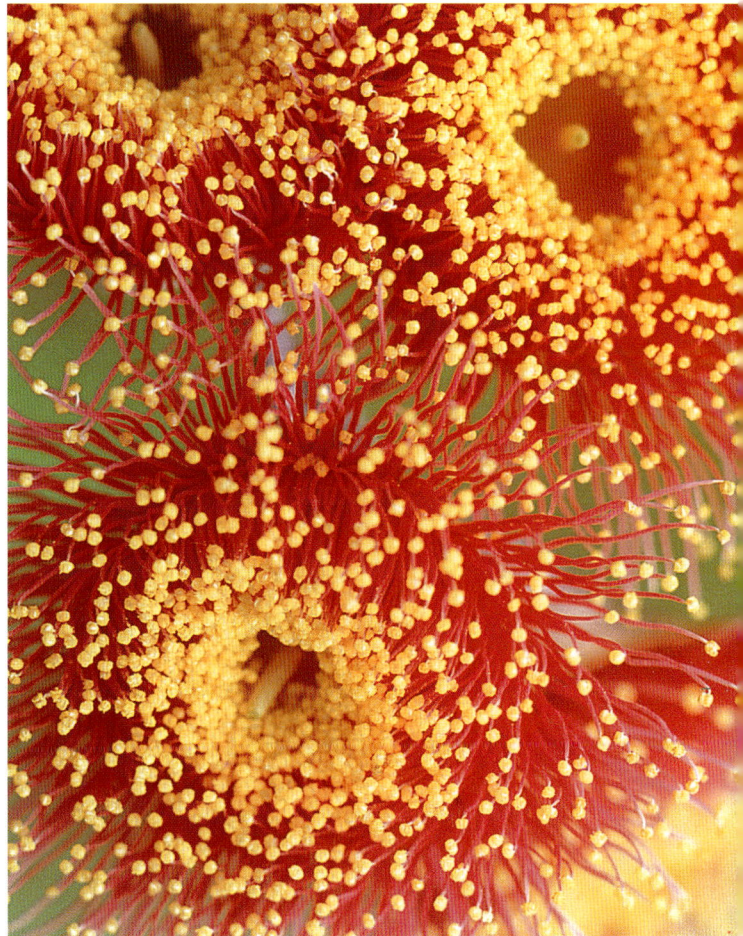

Gungurru, *Eucalyptus caesia.*

Waratah, *Telopea speciosissima.*

Southern Cross, *Xanthosia rotundifolia.*

King Spider Orchid, *Caladenia huegelii.*

Scarlet Banksia, *Banksia coccinea.*

Green Birdflower, *Crotalaria cunninghamii*.

A Crimson Rosella feasting on a grevillea flower spike.

A male Long-billed Black-Cockatoo perches on the flower of a Bull Banksia, *Banksia grandis*.

Wherever you find wildflowers in rich profusion, you will find varied and abundant wildlife. Many birds and small mammals rely on the pollen and nectar for food, and smaller birds nest in bushy shrubs close to a source of food. Others eat the seeds and fruit when they develop, and yet others eat the insects that swarm around the flowers and ripe fruits.

But that is not the end of it. Where birds and their eggs and small mammals are in plenty, so will larger predators be in plenty. Birds such as owls and kookaburras, birds of prey, and lizards, goannas and snakes, quolls, dingos, and, sadly, introduced species such as feral cats and foxes, all seek the smaller creatures that are their sources of food.

The connections in the web of life are many and complex.

A New Holland Honeyeater probes the flower of an Albany Bottlebrush, *Callistemon glaucus.*

Pygmy-possums lick nectar from Coast Banksia, *Banksia integrifolia*.

A Sugar Glider sniffs a banksia flower.

A grasshopper investigates a Lotus Lily, *Nelumbo nucifera*.

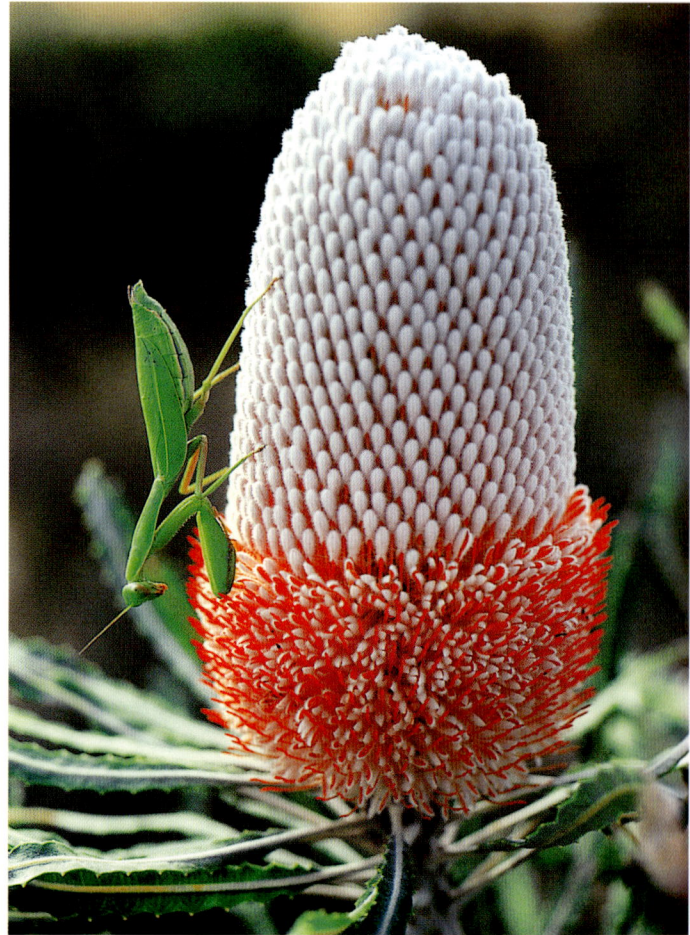

A mantid lurks on an Orange Banksia, *Banksia prionotes*, waiting for prey.

Bees, both social and solitary, and butterflies are probably the animals best known as pollinators of flowers.

Many parrots such as this female Red-tailed Black-Cockatoo rely on flowering and seeding trees and shrubs for survival.

Turn a simple flower, such as a daisy, any way you like – every angle is beautiful.

Like so much of our natural heritage, Australia's wildflowers need our care and protection if we are to continue enjoying their beauty and diversity. Australia's national parks and nature reserves are extensive, and the Parks and Wildlife Services do a mighty job in protecting our landscape, flora and fauna. Some commercial companies and non-government associations buy land to conserve its natural values or organise clean-ups of rubbish and pollution.

But we can all do more. Ironically, the gene pools of some of our most beautiful plant species are threatened by our love for them. Often new, hybrid forms are bred with brighter colours, larger blooms, longer flowering seasons and tolerance for a wider range of climates. The danger is that these forms have less genetic diversity than the originals and, being hardier, they can take over. This makes the integrity of the habitats in our parks and reserves of prime importance – otherwise the natural form of many species may be lost.

VARIOUS REGIONAL TITLES AVAILABLE
WHY NOT VISIT OUR WEBSITE FOR FURTHER DETAILS?

www.steveparish.com.au

Australia from the Heart
INTERACTIVE
CD-ROM

FEATURES

- IBM and Mac compatible
- Over 150 images in each CD
- Nature video – 9 minutes of video introduced and filmed by Steve Parish
- Stereo soundtrack – high quality, original music
- Slide show – 8 minutes of breathtaking images set to music
- Desktop images – full screen in three standard sizes
- Screen saver – Steve's best Australian images
- E-greetings – e-mail or print
- Clip art – 24 Steve Parish images to share
- Storybook – with images, prose, music and poetry
- Photo tips – dozens of photography secrets from the master himself
- Steve's autobiography

From an early age, Steve Parish has been driven by his undying passion for Australia to photograph every aspect of it, from its wild animals and plants to its many wild places. Then he began to turn his camera on Australians and their ways of life. This body of work forms one of Australia's most diverse photographic libraries. Over the years, these images of Australia have been used in thousands of publications, from cards, calendars and stationery to books – pictorial, reference, guide and children's. Steve has combined his considerable talents as a photographer, writer, poet and public speaker with his acute sense of needs in the marketplace to create a publishing company that today is recognised world wide.

Steve's primary goal is to turn the world on to nature, and, in pursuit of this lifelong objective, he has published a world-class range of children's books and learning aids. He sees our children as the decision makers of tomorrow and the guardians of our heritage.

Steve Parish
PUBLISHING

Published by Steve Parish Publishing Pty Ltd

PO Box 1058, Archerfield, Queensland 4108 Australia

www.steveparish.com.au

© copyright Steve Parish Publishing Pty Ltd

ISBN 174021084 0

Photography: Steve Parish

Text: Cath Jones, Wynne Webber

Cover design: Audra Colless

Cover photograph: Finke River Mallee, *Eucalyptus sessilis*

Printed in Hong Kong by South China Printing Co. Ltd

Film by Inprint Pty Ltd, Australia

Designed and produced in Australia at the Steve Parish Publishing Studios